JOSEPH HAYDN

KONZERT

für Violine und Orchester / for Violin and Orchestra

G-Dur / G Major

Hoboken VIIa: 4

Violin and Orchestra PAGE 1

Part for Violin PAGE 21

ALLEGRO EDITIONS

Published in 2022 by Allegro Editions

Concerto No. 4 in G Major for Violin and Orchestra
ISBN: 978-1-64837-272-8 (paperback)

Cover design by Kaitlyn Whitaker

Cover image: *Black and White Piano Illustration* by Nerthuz, courtesy of iStock;
Violin front view, by AGCuesta, courtesy of Shutterstock

A Word on the Work

Haydn composed four violin concertos during his lifetime, which have become an essential part of the violin repertoire. They are considered masterpieces of the classical era and showcase Haydn's skill as a composer.

The first violin concerto in C major was composed in the 1760s and is believed to be the earliest surviving concerto for the instrument. It consists of three movements, including an opening allegro, a slow and lyrical adagio, and a lively finale in the form of a rondo. The concerto is characterized by its elegant melodies, delicate ornamentation, and virtuosic passages, particularly in the first movement.

Haydn's second violin concerto in G major was composed in the late 1760s or early 1770s. Like the first concerto, it consists of three movements, with a lively allegro as the opening movement, a slow and expressive adagio, and a spirited rondo as the final movement. The concerto is notable for its rhythmic vitality and the contrast between the solo violin and the accompanying orchestra.

The third violin concerto in A major is one of Haydn's most popular works for the violin. Composed in the mid-1770s, it has four movements, including a lively allegro moderato, a tender adagio, a minuet and trio, and a virtuosic finale in the form of a rondo. The concerto is notable for its elegance and charm, as well as its use of ornamentation and virtuosic flourishes.

Haydn's final violin concerto in G major was composed in the late 1780s or early 1790s. It has three movements, with a sparkling allegro moderato as the opening movement, a lyrical adagio, and a lively rondo. The concerto is known for its technical demands and its use of double stops and other advanced techniques.

Haydn's violin concertos are masterpieces of the classical era and continue to be performed by violinists throughout the world. They showcase Haydn's skill as a composer and his ability to write music that is both elegant and virtuosic.

JOSEPH HAYDN

KONZERT

für Violine und Orchester / for Violin and Orchestra

G-Dur / G major

Hob. VIIa: 4

Herausgegeben von / Edited by
Ferdinand Küchler

Kadenzen vom Herausgeber / Cadenzas by the editor

KONZERT
für Violine und Orchester

Konzert für Violine und Orchester

Konzert für Violine und Orchester

Violine und Orchester

Konzert für Violine und Orchester

Violine und Orchester

Violine und Orchester

Konzert für Violine und Orchester

JOSEPH HAYDN

KONZERT

für Violine / for Violin

G-Dur / G major

Hob. VIIa: 4

Herausgegeben von / Edited by
Ferdinand Küchler

Kadenzen vom Herausgeber / Cadenzas by the editor

KONZERT
für Violine

*) Alle Tutti sind mitzuspielen | *) All "tuttis" should be played | *) Les Tutti doivent tous être joués

Violine

28 Konzert für Violine und Orchester

www.ingramcontent.com/pod-product-compliance
Lightning Source LLC
Chambersburg PA
CBHW041437040426
42453CB00021B/2454